BEAUTY AND THE BEAST
AND
THE LION AND THE CARPENTER

BEAUTY

AND

THE BEAST

Once upon a time there lived a very rich merchant who had three pretty daughters. They lived in a beautiful house and had many servants to look after them.

The youngest daughter was the prettiest of them all and was called Beauty. She was also very kind and good. Her two elder sisters were pretty, but they were neither kind nor good.

One day their father came home looking very worried and sad. When his daughters asked him what was the matter, he replied that he had lost his fortune. They would have to sell their lovely house and go to live in a cottage in the country.

The elder sisters were very angry when they heard this news, but Beauty thought how nice it would be to live in the country surrounded by the woods and fields. So the merchant found a little cottage and he and his family all went to live there.

Beauty was very happy and worked all day in the house and garden. Her elder sisters, however, grumbled all the time because they had to work and no longer had pretty clothes and jewels to wear.

Their father grew fruit and vegetables in his garden to make enough money for his family to live comfortably.

One day, after the family had lived in their cottage for about a year, the merchant told his daughters that he had to go to a distant town on business. He said that he may not return until the next day. He promised that he would bring them each a gift and asked them what they would like. The elder daughters asked for jewels and satin dresses, but all Beauty wanted was for her father to return home safely. When he said that she must have a gift she asked for a bunch of red roses. As their father rode away on horseback, Beauty stood at the door of the cottage and waved to him.

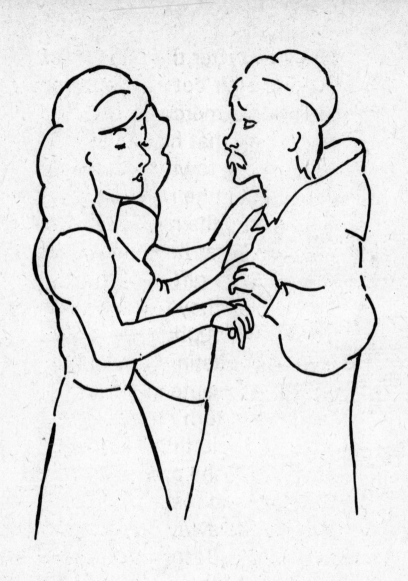

When the merchant had finished his business in town, he set off on the long journey home. After he had been riding for some time he began to feel tired and cold. By now, he was in the middle of a dense wood and thought that he was lost. He longed to find somewhere to rest. Then suddenly he came to a place in the woods where the trees cleared and formed a long avenue.

He dismounted from his horse and struggled on foot through the deep snow to the entrance of the long avenue, and could see in the distance, a large building that looked like a Palace. His horse followed him until they reached the end of the avenue where they found before them a really magnificent Palace.

There was no one in sight so he took his horse round the back of the Palace and found the stables. He then fed it and left it to rest in these comfortable surroundings.

When he returned to the front of the Palace he noticed that the door was open so he climbed the steps and walked in. As he entered the hall he saw that one of the doors leading off was open. It seemed as though the whole place was deserted so he entered the room and was delighted by the sight which met his eyes.

This was the Dining Room
and the table was fully
prepared with every kind of
food you can imagine. As he
was hungry after his long and
hard journey he could not
resist eating some of the food
and soon had a full stomach.
This made him feel tired so he
wandered off in search of
somewhere to rest.

He soon came across a magnificent bedroom with an enormous fire blazing in the grate, and a large bed with huge pillows. Not having seen anyone in the Palace he decided to sleep and continue his search of the Palace in the morning.

When morning arrived, the merchant woke to find the table already prepared for breakfast, which he ate quickly and then set out to find whoever was living in the Palace.

His search eventually led him outside the Palace and he was pleased to discover it had stopped snowing. He was, however, unaware that he was being watched.

On his way through the grounds he saw a beautiful rose garden. This reminded him of Beauty's request for some red roses so he went to gather a bunch for her. He had only broken off one rose when he heard a terrible roar behind him. On turning round, he saw that it was a horrible Beast.

The Beast was very angry
with the merchant for eating
his food and sleeping in his
bed, and then repaying this
kindness by stealing the
roses. Beauty's father
explained that they were a
present for his daughter and
so the Beast said that he
would spare his life on the
condition that one of his
daughters came to live at the
Palace.

The merchant reluctantly agreed to this plan and set off for home. The three sisters were pleased to see their father but they soon realised that he was very unhappy.

When he told them what had happened they were all very upset. Naturally, none of the sisters wanted to leave home and live with an ugly Beast. However, because her father had made a promise, Beauty said that she would go. After four weeks had passed, her father, very sadly, took Beauty back to the Palace and left her outside.

Beauty spent a long time wandering round outside the Palace before she dared to enter. She admired the gardens and trees and the Palace looked really beautiful; and deserted.

Time passed and eventually she plucked up enough courage to enter the Palace and found to her surprise the tables were laid with food, and fires were blazing in every room.

The Beast was watching her all the time and eventually they met. As her father had told her what to expect, she was not too frightened of the Beast and told him she was at the Palace to fulfil her father's promise.

Beauty lived at the Palace quite happily for several months. There was everything she could wish for to make life happy and comfortable. She amused herself during the day, but every evening the Beast joined her for supper, and they soon became great friends.

Each night, however, the Beast would ask Beauty to marry him and her answer was always the same. She was very fond of the Beast but she could not marry him. He became sadder and sadder and this upset Beauty very much but she kept telling herself she could not possibly marry a Beast.

Whenever Beauty walked in the garden, which she did nearly every day when the weather was fine, the Beast would suddenly appear and present to her one of his precious roses. At first he would not tell her why he did this, but eventually admitted it was a sign of his love for her.

Although she was quite happy at the Palace, Beauty did not forget her father. She still longed to see him. One morning when she looked into the mirror she saw a picture of her father lying ill in bed. This worried Beauty very much and she cried all day, longing for the evening when the Beast would come to her.

When he did arrive and saw how sad she looked he asked her what the trouble was. Beauty told him of the picture she had seen in the mirror and asked the Beast to let her return home. The Beast did not like to see her so unhappy, so he agreed, and Beauty promised to come back to him after she had seen her father.

The next morning when
Beauty was ready to return to
her old home, the Beast gave
her a ring. He told her to blow
on it if she wanted to return
to him and she would
immediately find herself back
at the Palace. He begged her
to come back to him and said
that he would die if she did
not return.

Of course, Beauty said that
she would not leave him for
any longer than necessary.
She just wanted to make sure
that her father was well. The
Beast then told her to blow on
the magic ring and straight
away she was back in the
cottage.

Beauty's father and sisters
were very happy and
surprised to see her. Her
father had not been well but
as soon as Beauty arrived he
began to feel better. They all
wanted to know how she
spent her time at the Palace
and whether the Beast was
good to her. The time passed
quickly and Beauty was very
happy to see her father return
to his usual self. She could
not believe that she had been
at home for two weeks.

Meanwhile, the poor Beast was very lonely. He thought that Beauty had left him forever and gradually he became more and more upset. He could not bear to go inside the Palace and spent his time in the gardens. He did not bother to eat now that he was alone and was starving himself to death. He grew weaker and weaker and eventually he collapsed under the trees. He lay there and just wanted to die.

Back at the cottage, however, Beauty knew that she could not stay much longer, but she was so happy to be back with her family.

Then one night she had a
terrible dream in which she
saw the Beast lying very still
under the trees.

She was so frightened by this,
that in the morning she
decided that she must return
to the Palace. The two elder
sisters and their father did not
want her to go but Beauty
could not bear to think of the
Beast alone and ill. She blew
on her magic ring and
immediately found herself
back at the Palace.
Beauty knew that the Beast
never came to see her until
evening and she spent the day
wandering from room to room
longing for him to appear.

Then at last it was evening
but there was still no sign of
the beast. Suddenly the
dreadful thought struck
Beauty that perhaps her
dream had been true and the
Beast was in the garden lying
ill. She ran as quickly as she
could out into the grounds of
the Palace and sure enough,
there was the poor Beast,
lying still as though he was
dead.

Beauty was overcome with
grief. She knelt down beside
him and said, "Oh my poor
Beast, if only you would get
better I will marry you. You
are so kind and good." She
then covered her face with
her hands and cried.

When she looked up the
Beast was nowhere to be
seen, but there was a very
handsome Prince by her side.

"Where is my Beast?" she
asked.

The Prince explained that a
wicked fairy had put a spell on
him and said that he must be
a Beast until a beautiful lady
was willing to marry him.
Then the spell would be
broken.

Beauty married her Prince and he arranged for her father and sisters to come to the Palace. They all lived happily ever after.

THE LION AND THE CARPENTER

There was an oasis in the Garden of Eden where every species of the animal world lived happily and free. Flowers, fruit, delicious food and pure water springs were at their disposal. Fortunately for them, Man had not yet arrived on the scene to disturb their peace and tranquility.

One night a duck had a most extraordinary dream. The Queen of the ducks appeared and told him that he must leave his home and travel towards the Orient for a hundred days and a hundred nights. She did not tell him why he had to go, nor what he would find when he got there.

The following morning when he awoke, the duck remembered his dream. He knew that he must obey the Queen's instructions to leave. After eating a hearty breakfast he began his long journey, first flying and then swimming.

As the days passed, the duck became very lonely and he longed for a companion. However, eventually his journey came to an end.

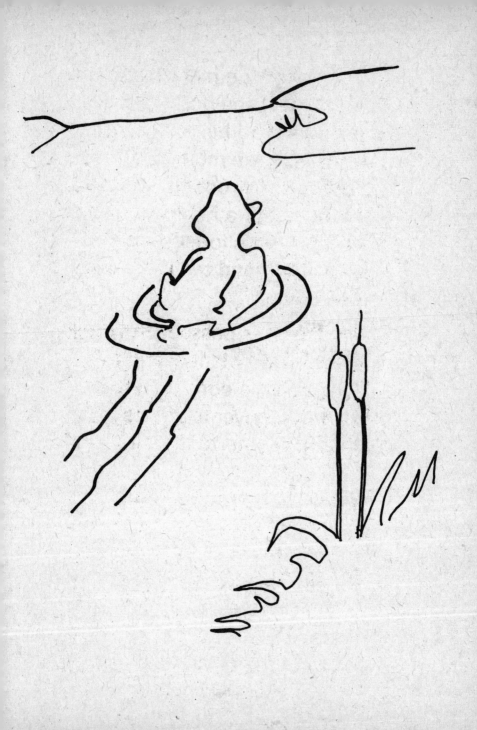

After travelling for a hundred days and nights the duck was very tired. He stopped to rest on a rock which was jutting out of the water. To his surprise he heard the Queen's voice. She scolded him and said that he had made a big mistake. Instead of travelling towards the East, as he had done, he should have travelled towards the West. However, now that he was here, he must stay and face a terrible creature: Man.

The Queen told the duck how Man was very cruel to all the other animals. He made them his slaves and sometimes he even killed them.

Naturally the duck was very
frightened and he began to
search for a place to hide
from the strange creature
called Man. He walked and
walked and eventually he
came to a cave where a
young lion cub was lying in
the sun. The duck was so
pleased to see another living
creature that he did not
hesitate in approaching the
lion.

The two animals soon became friends. The duck told the lion about his long journey and how he had made a mistake by travelling in the wrong direction. In turn, the lion explained that he was alone in the world. He thought his parents had been captured by Man and was determined to avenge this deed. He had decided the only way to do this was to fight man.

The duck also wanted to live in peace so he promised to help the lion to unite all the animals of the forest in order to fight against Man. Having agreed on their plan, the two friends decided to go to sleep, and they would begin their fight for survival against Man the next day.

When morning came, the two friends did, indeed, begin their task. They set off into the forest to search for the other animals. It was not easy for the little duck to keep in step with the lion who was so much bigger.

After a while a four-legged
animal appeared in front of
them. He said that he was a
donkey and was running away
from Man. This creature
called Man wanted to make
him his slave and the donkey
knew he would have to work
very hard and would probably
be given very little to eat in
return. He also knew that he
would be treated cruelly in
other ways.

The lion told the donkey that
he was organising an army
against Man, made up of all
the animals of the forest. The
donkey was very interested
and asked if he could join.
The lion was very pleased to
have the donkey in his army
and gave him the rank of
corporal.

The three animals continued on into the forest and soon they met another four-legged creature who called himself a horse. He, also, was running away from Man and was very glad to meet with the three friends.

The horse told how Man had the habit of jumping on his back and making him gallop very fast. At other times, Man would make him pull a heavy cart and if he dared to stop, he was beaten with a stick.

The other three animals were horrified at this and told the horse about the army they were forming. He willingly agreed to join them.

The lion continued to march, followed by the other three members of the army. Eventually they came upon yet another four legged animal but this one had two humps on his back. He said he was a camel and that he was trying to avoid a strange creature called Man.

The camel related how frightened he was of Man, who wanted to make him his slave. The lion asked just how strong Man was and the camel replied that the lion was certainly stronger than Man, but the problem was not one of strength.

The fact remained that Man was so cunning he always managed to win because of this. This made the lion more determined than ever to overcome Man and so he asked the camel if he would like to join their army.

The camel agreed and so joined the other animals who intended to help the lion in his battle against Man. So the small army, with the lion in front, set out once again in their search for Man.

The lion decided to confront
this strange creature but the
donkey and the rest of the
animals were afraid. In fact, it
was Man, a carpenter, who
after seeing the lion decided
to capture him. In order to do
this, Man had to use his
cunning. He told the lion that
he was ill and wondered
whether the lion could help
him get well.

The lion was naturally very flattered to be asked for his assistance. He decided that this creature had realised how intelligent the lion was, so he agreed to help. The carpenter explained how unhappy he was because Man made him work day and night.

On hearing this, the lion was more determined than ever to find Man and kill him.

The lion asked the carpenter what he intended to do with the wooden boards. He said that he was going to make a wooden box in which the panther could hide whenever Man was nearby.

The panther was a fierce animal with sharp claws and the carpenter was extremely frightened of him. He was quite desperate because if the box was not ready soon, the panther would tear him to pieces.

The lion thought that if anyone should have a place to hide from Man it should be himself. After all, he was the king of the forest! He persuaded the carpenter to make the box for him by pinning him against a tree with his paws.

The carpenter was secretly
very pleased, as this had been
his plan all along. He thought
himself very clever. He had
not said who he was, the lion
still did not know that he was
actually Man. He had
convinced the lion to have a
hiding place built by
pretending that he also was
afraid. The carpenter was
keen to begin building the box
and it would soon be obvious
why he was so anxious that it
should be the strongest box
he had ever made.

So the carpenter began to
work. He invited the lion to
inspect the box. It must be
large enough and have plenty
of air holes. The lion got
inside the box and tried to
make himself comfortable. It
was a tight squeeze!

The carpenter's plan had worked. As soon as the lion was inside the box he fastened the lid down with some nails that were so large that not even a lion would be able to open it.

The lion, who had not understood what was happening, asked to be let out.

The carpenter said he was sorry but he had no intention of releasing an animal who wanted to kill Man-himself. He had proved that Man was so cunning he was able to capture the king of the forest who was so much stronger than himself. It had only taken the use of a very simple trap.

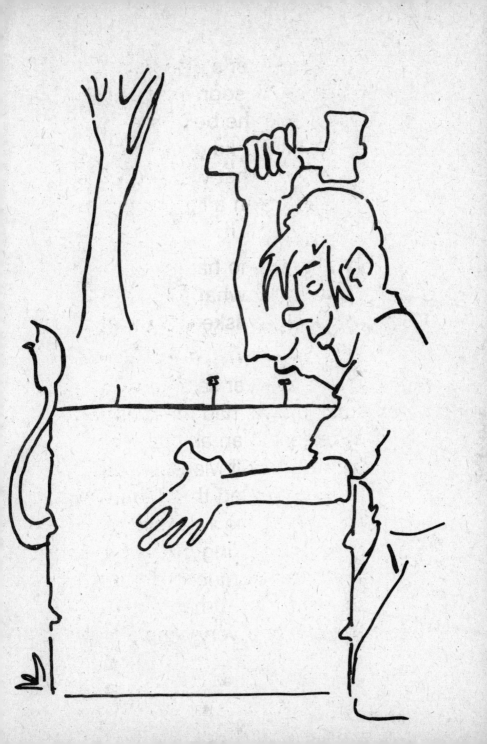

This left the lion with no choice but to call for his army. They were extremely sad that their friend had been trapped in such a way. The lion told them that he had been very foolish to think that he could outwit Man and he had decided to abandon his plan to avenge his parents. They had no alternative but to disband their army.

They all agreed to go their separate ways. The donkey would return to pulling carts, the horse would return to galloping with his master, the camel would return to the desert and wait for a caravan with which he could work, and lastly the duck would return from where he had come. At least he believed that he would be free of Man there.

Printed in the USSR
for the Publishers Peter Haddock Ltd.
Bridlington, England